Table Of C<

C000135851

Chapter 1) Sand, Gravel, And Concrete - Setting The Foundation

Hey there, first before we get started, I'd like to set the stage for this book. Throughout the course of this you'll find little dialog, and a lot of straightforward information about spreading your brand or message through the most popular place on the planet – Facebook. As you go through this book, keep an open mind, as I'm going to break many of the "rules" taught when it comes to Facebook. Everything in here is based off of facts, in the trenches testing, and years of full-time marketing on Facebook. This book will ruffle some feathers, and change the way you think about social media.

Why Listen To Me?

With all the noise out there about how facebook works, you need to learn from someone who is in the trenches every day tweaking and testing things. And you need to be able to see how every aspect of it works, paid advertising, viral traffic, apps, and true word of mouth marketing. Over the last 2 years I've taught 10's of thousands of marketers how to crush it online with facebook. I have had many of fan pages with millions of people talking about it.

Here, take a glance at my facebook insights statistics.

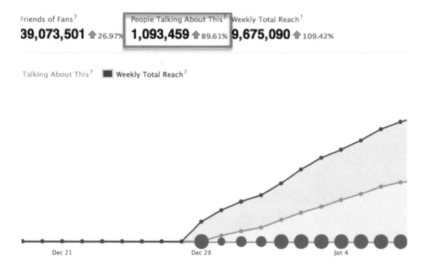

(If that looks confusing, no worries, you'll be a facebook ninja master before you get finished with this book... it basically means over one million people are actively talking about my page or brand)

The best part of that stat isn't the fact that I'm reaching over a million people, it's that I did it from zero in about 3 weeks. And that's because I have a core knowledge of what works with PPC combined with what it takes to go viral long-term.

(Note: As of the time writing this, I'm generating way over 1 million hits of laser targeted traffic to my offers every week. If you'd like to find out more about me and my other books on traffic and sales-funnels head on over to: http://marketingwithdon.com)

Setting The Foundation

There are many different types of pages that you can create within Facebook. Local pages, business pages, pages for actors, websites, and just about anything you can think of. And how you set up your page from day one is absolutely critical. Do it wrong… and Facebook will yank your page right out from under you. (There will be NOTHING you can do to get it back)

So… you may be thinking - How can I set up my fan page so that it's secure in any situation?

Well, I'm glad you asked.

In every single case (except for a local business) the best way to set up a fan page on facebook is to set it up as a "website". To do this all you have to do is go to www.facebook.com/pages/create.php and once you get there you will be able to choose what kind of page you're setting up. Now, depending on how facebook looks (they change the layout here and there) you'll find 6 big box options to choose from. Over on the top right there will be a group called "brand or product". Go ahead and select that, then you'll be met with the ability to select a sub-category. Once there, from the drop down box select "website". Then you pick a name for your page and enter it in the dialog box and you're set.

You now have a facebook page that is safe, secure, and ready for traffic.

Chapter 2) Timeline Tactics

So, now you've got your page set-up and you're almost ready to start driving traffic over to it. But, before you start getting all "gung-ho" on buying traffic, setting up ads, or trying to go viral, you need to get the "visual layout" of your page looking great. The first thing that people see when they land on your page is the timeline, if it doesn't look good, then you will have lost any chance of getting a fan on your page.

Putting The Timeline Into Perspective

Imagine that it's a Tuesday morning at about 7am and you wake up with the most excruciating back pain you have ever had. You know that you desperately need to go to a chiropractor, but the problem is that you're on a trip and your normal doctor isn't around. So you do a quick little search and find a local Chiropractor in town. You call them up, speak to the receptionist, and book an emergency appointment for noon. The day goes by, you're in pain all day. Then, at about 11:45am you show up to the chiropractors office ready to get worked on, and a little relief from the shooting pain you've been experiencing all day. When you walk in an odor hits your nose that is so strong that you almost gag while you walk in.

You Immediately Regret Picking This Dr.'s Office

This is how it is with your fan page. When a new potential lead "walks in your door" everything needs to be in order. You need to have a friendly cover page, certain posts should be pinned across the timeline, milestones should be there, and it should scream "WE ARE SAFE!"

Before I ever start driving traffic to a fan page, I set up a timeline cover, and I add at least 4 posts to the page that are extremely engaging. Let your timeline cover establish the brand, and let your posts engage your traffic and give your page a trusting feel.

Great Timeline Cover Example

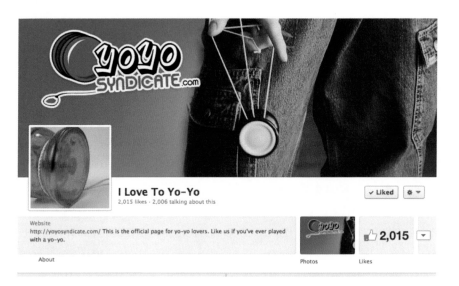

See how the logo is very clear in the photo along with a very welcoming photo that should resonate with the traffic that lands there. The target of this audience is obviously a younger group of people so you can see why that's the photo we chose.

Great Post To Start With Example

(Status update reads: "Have You Yo-Yoed Yet Today? (yes/no)... vote below")

Now these may not be "huge" numbers, but by I get clicks to this page for pennies, build a brand, and generate massive goodwill in the marketplace that I'm building a business in. So when you're starting up a campaign, do take some time to set up some engagement posts, and have a nice and friendly timeline cover up.

(Note: To get some free timeline covers for your niche, business, or clients head on over to: http://marketingwithdon.com/bookgift/ and you can download some for free. Unique, proven, and professionally designed by my in-house graphics team)

Chapter 3) One Penny Clicks - (in today's world)

It's time to get to the good stuff – insane traffic, for cheap. This chapter is going to be all about Pay Per Click (PPC) advertising from within the facebook platform. Most people in the world will never understand how to do this right. (It's because everyone does it wrong)

Fact: The fastest way into any NEW market is to pay for traffic.

People talk about partnering into a market, they talk about going viral, or hooking into a trend, and while all of these can work, time and time again I've found that paying for traffic is the fastest way into just about any market.

Myth: Every subscriber is worth $1.00/mo

This is a myth that I have found to be rampant in the Internet marketing community. I'm not sure who started saying this first, but it couldn't be any further from the truth. People are not numbers, and you can't blanket them with a $/mo value based on how many numbers you have on your list, or your fan page. How much your fan base, or subscriber base is worth per month is based on the amount of value you can provide to their life.

Here's an example.

Say you're in the dog niche, and you're also in the real estate niche. Which one of these pieces of information would you be willing to pay more for?

> **Dog Niche:** Training on how to potty train your dog so it doesn't pee in the house anymore.

> **Real Estate Niche:** Training on how to sell your (or someone else's) home to avoid bankruptcy or make money.

So when you logically think about it, there is just no way that a 1,000 person dog training list or fan page will ever generate the same amount of revenue as a 1,000 person real estate focused list.

So, we know that paying for traffic is the absolute fastest way to enter a market or spread your message, but not all traffic is created equal. So before I give you examples of how I've gotten one cent clicks over and over, realize that is not where the bar should be set. You're not looking for the cheapest clicks possible. You're looking to buy clicks that have the highest Return On Investment (ROI) possible.

Let's dig in.

One Penny Clicks Example – Pit Bull Puppies

7,617 Clicks | **7,100** Actions | **0.639%** CTR | **$92.56** Spent | **$0.08** CPM | **$0.01** CPC

Impressions ?	Social Impressions ?	Social % ?	Clicks ?	Social Clicks ?	CTR ?	Social CTR ?	CPC ?	CPM ?	Spent ?	Reach ?	Frequ ?
674,097	60,834	9.02%	5,115	433	0.759%	0.712%	0.01	0.07	$50.00	45,020	15.0
518,157	89,987	17.37%	2,502	419	0.483%	0.466%	0.02	0.08	$42.56	39,182	13.2

Now to get clicks in this volume a couple things need to happen.

You need a high CTR – A click through ratio is going to determine a lot of things. It decides how often facebook is going to show your ad. (which is what the frequency column represents) Facebook wants to train people to click their ads, it's how they make money, so if you have an ad that is getting lots of clicks when people see it, then you're going to get rewarded with a higher frequency.

Deep Targeting – There is an entire chapter on this later, so for now, let's just say that there is a reason I targeted German Shepherds and not "dogs" for an interest. (in some cases, you do want to broaden... we will get to that more later)

Similar Niche With A Higher ROI – German Shepherd Dogs

Now, here's a niche that isn't quite as viral, but it's still a good niche. When you go into a niche, you need to come armed with all of the right information. So the first thing you need is to research the audience, know who they are, how much money they make, and what they are interested in.

My first research step is to go over to Google and just type in a keyword related to my niche. I search for "German Shepherd Dog" in Google, glance at the top 10 and see gsdca.org

So I head on over to Quantcast.com (which is a free research tool) and type in their URL.

As you can see, they have above average income, and they are mainly middle-aged women.

This is good – you want people with money, who are willing to spend it.

Now, on the other hand, here's what the top pit bulls website returned.

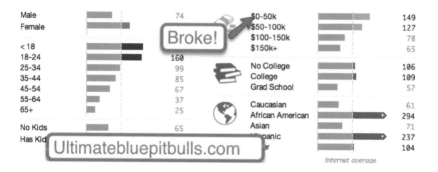

So, even though I paid a little more for the clicks in the German shepherd niche, it was ok, because they have the money to spend with me once I get them onto my page and into my sales funnels.

Now, before we go too much further I want to add that there are two extremely different types of ad campaigns. There are "like" campaigns, and there are buyer campaigns. These are both completely different, and we need to cover them before going any further.

Like Campaign Example

This campaign is meant to do one thing, and one thing only – get likes. There are a few different ways to pull this off, but what is really at work here is the fact that it looks like nothing else on the wall. I make sure and use short, punchy ad copy that looks like a status update and not an ad. Most ads on the wall use every last bit of text that they can, but I stick out by having my ad look nothing like everyone else's.

So remember, on like campaigns: have a solid call to action telling the user to "like" the ad (this way they click the "like" button instead of the link at the top – this instantly makes them a fan of your page), make it short, punchy, and like a status update, and use an extremely social photo.

Here's Another Example

Politics Suck

Agree? Then "like" us!

You like Politics Suck.

View on Site · Create a Similar Ad

As you can see, I did this one a little different. Instead of using all the ad-copy, I referred to the title of the page in the copy. This effectively shortened it to a one liner, which always sticks out on the side of the facebook wall.

Here's One Last Example

Pit Bulls

Click "like" if i'm CUTE!

You like Pit Bulls.

View on Site · Create a Similar Ad

Referring to the photo is a great way to switch out ads on like campaigns over time to avoid banner-blindness.

(Note: banner-blindness is when you see the same photo on your wall as an ad over and over and you become immune to it and tune it out, the same thing also happens with a status update, that is why here and there we try switching out our ad photos and ad-copy ever so slightly)

Now before we go any further, I want you to know that one penny clicks aren't the norm. If you're doing something local you're pretty much never going to get them, and most niches will never get close to one cent either. One cent is special, and the niche has to fit the viral criteria.

Viral Criteria

Is It Big Enough?
Is It Evergreen?
Is There Passion?
Is There A Sense Of Community?
Is There Controversy?

Now if you don't want to do all the viral marketing or even worry about maintaining a fan page you can direct affiliate promote from the ad system. Here's an example of a buyer campaign I did for a business partner of mine's Wordpress plug-in launch.

Buyer Campaign

As you can see here I am very up-front about everything. I tell people what it does, do a very red sign for the ad so that people notice it inside of the blue FB world., tell the price, and give a call to action to click. The main thing that makes this ad different is that when you do CPC you are paying for actual clicks and not impressions. This means that unless they click, you don't have to pay. This is powerful because when you're up-front that it's a "buy" or purchase and the price, people that aren't ready to spend that money won't be clicking your ad.

Chapter 4) Deep Targeting

Now that you've been introduced to paid traffic and know that getting cheap clicks is possible, it's time to dive deep into how to get those clicks and how to cheapen your clicks no matter what niche you go in.

Myth: You want as many clicks as possible.

This may be a little difficult to wrap your head around at first, but this is an important concept to understand.

Getting lots of clicks is nice, but the way facebook actually works is that the higher the Click Through Ratio (CTR) of your ads, the less you'll pay for clicks, and the more clicks they are going to give you. The mistake people make is that they chose broad targets instead of deep, laser precise targeting.

Deep Targeting Example 1 - MMA Niche

First, let's start with the typical ad that people will choose.

Ad

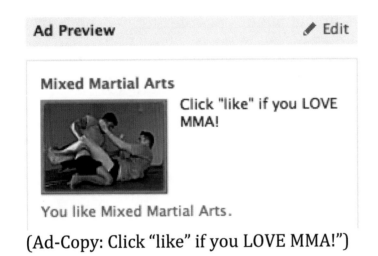

(Ad-Copy: Click "like" if you LOVE MMA!")

Targeting

(Targeting: MMA, Brazilian Jiu Jitsu, Thai Boxing or Muay Thai)

Now this ad isn't terrible, but it could be dialed in a LOT better. There are only a few interests, and they are very general. There are no famous people targeted, no brands, and only 5 interests targeted total.

Here's and example of a more dialed in ad.

(That may be hard to see, but those are all names of MMA fighters)

Now, here's the ad that is not only going to get you cheaper clicks, but you'll get more of them!

As you can see, this ad is targeting fighters that are in the niche, along with different fighting styles, and even the person who owns a fighting company. This is a great ad. The only problem though is if you wanted to go after this niche, and weren't into mixed martial arts, you wouldn't know any of these interests. And that is WHY it works. Only people who are passionate about MMA will know these people or interests. So when you target the interest, you know it's only landing on the wall of the most passionate people, and not the wall of someone who has only seen one MMA fight.

I really don't know anything about MMA, but yet I'm in the niche. I don't know anything about German Shepherds either, but I'm in the niche.

How?

Well, glad you asked.

There are 2 methods I use to find only the best interests in a new niche on facebook. Both of them are free, and almost NOBODY is using either one of them.

Deep Targeting Method 1 – The "Celebrity Tree"

The way this works is by understanding that celebrities are one of the best ways to find targeted people in a niche. The problem though, is once celebrities get to "mainstream" people will like them as an interest on facebook that are not passionate about a niche. Take Lance Armstrong for an example if you're trying to target the cyclist niche. Obviously anyone passionate about the niche will have him as an interest, but so will many people that have absolutely no interest in cycling. I know who he is, but don't care about cycling at all. Ever heard of Tom Jelte Slagter? Me either, but he was the top cyclist in 2013 and a perfect interest on facebook.

Basically how this whole "Celebrity Tree" thing works is by starting with a very generic interest, and building a tree based on celebrities in the niche or lateral interests.

MMA Deep Targeting Tree Example

The "Celebrity Tree" method is great for not only finding amazing interests, it's but also great for dialing in ads for cheaper costs. This way you can test generic things like "MMA" and if it looks like there could be some good, or cheap traffic there, you can start up a tree, and dial in the cheapest interests possible.

Another simple way to find deep targeting is by using another free research tool. The Google Keyword Tool is something that is mainly used by marketers for Search

Engine Optimization (SEO). Usually these 2 types of marketing don't mix that much as SEO takes a lot longer to get going than PPC or viral traffic. But, the keyword tool will help you discover great "long tail" keywords by simply spying on your competitors.

Deep Targeting Method 2 – Long-Tail Interests – Bodybuilding Example

Say we you are going after the health and fitness niche. So you head on over to Google.com and search for "bodybuilding" and find that the first site that comes up is bodybuilding.com. Now the first thing you should do is take bodybuilding.com over to quantcast.com and figure out what the age demographics is for the page. Once you've got the demographics written down, it's time to get sneaky. Head on over to the keyword tool, and enter in bodybuilding.com

You'll find something similar to this.

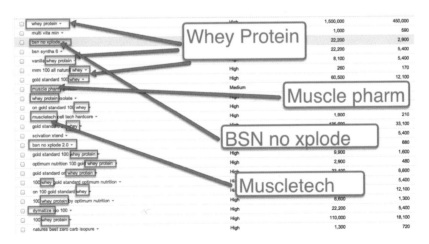

So as you can see, if I knew absolutely nothing about bodybuilding I could easily do a quick 60 seconds worth of research and have all the laser targeting I could ever need. Targeting doesn't have to be hard; most people just go around "guessing". Don't do that. Take a few moments out, build a celebrity tree, research the market, then run your campaign.

Chapter 5) Critical Controversy

Controversy is what separates the great pages from the EPIC pages. Pit bulls for example goes insanely viral because of the controversy in the niche. People are always commenting away on everything that gets posted. The same goes with controversial topics that happen to be trending at all. Watch for when something happens at a predictable event with mass coverage. The Olympics happen at a predictable time every 4 years, and there is always bound to be a controversial trend you can hook in to.

Then, there is taking controversy to the extreme level. I see pages popping up like this in the millions of fans everywhere. Using either controversial based names, or viral phrase names.

Controversial Based Name Example 1

1-800 Choke Dat Hoe
915,975 likes · 1,455,448 talking about this

Movie
This page is a *quote* from "Madea's Big Happy Family"! We post funny/quote photos, give us a like and we'll entertain you. If you do not like something we post please send us a message. Thanks.

(Name: 1-800 Choke Dat Hoe - Yep, that's 1.4 million "talking about this")

This is a phrase out of "Madea's Big Happy Family" that has been turned into a viral page. You could take this page and profit by sending the traffic to CPA offers like iPhone giveaways. (profiting from fan pages is a whole different book, we won't go there today)

Controversial Based Name Example 2

heralds new discoveries, is not 'eureka!' but 'that's funny...' -Isaac Asimov

I fucking love science
2,789,176 likes · 4,497,007 talking about this

✓ Liked   Message

Science Website
We're here for the science – the funny side of science. Quotes, jokes, memes, photography and anything your admin finds awesome and strange. If our name

IT'S A VIRUS!

👍 2.7m

Top Fans

NEUROSCIENCE 2012

About   Photos   Likes   Top Fans   Events

(Name: I fucking love science - 2.7 million "likers" and 4.49 million talking about this page weekly!!)

This is one of the most popular pages on facebook. I watch it all the time and so do most of the facebook students I coach. They have some of the most well thought out, and viral, photos online.

Viral Phrase Name Example 1

(Name: Never cry for the one who don't deserve ur tears – Another 1.3 million+ fans off of a viral phrase name)

Viral Phrase Name Example 2

(Name: A relationship is not a test so why cheat? – 1.7 million "likes" and 2.4+ million "talking about this viral phrase)

This is just another example of a page with an insane amount of traffic. Just to let this hit home, here are a few more: *"I miss you more when you don't text me"*, *"I hate getting up for school"*, and *"I'm sooo sick of politics"*.

Now the reason these work, is that when someone hit's "like" or "share" on these photo's the name that goes out on their timeline is so controversial that people are compelled to click. (If you go after building these types of pages, set up an official site along with it and brand your page to that website so that facebook doesn't shut your page down)

So as you can see, controversy is a critical component to going viral. If your niche doesn't have it in general, then create it. When posting, talk about two big companies, and ask for people's opposing viewpoints, that will get your posts going far more viral.

Chapter 6) Over-post Myth-busting

This is a myth that is so big amongst even some big facebook marketers. And this may be against everything you've ever been taught, but I have tons of facts and data to back this up.

> **Myth:** You should only post a few times a day, not to annoy your fans

Over years of testing, I've concluded that posting hourly (during the day of your target audience) will get your message out further in almost every single case than sparingly posting.

Here's Why

When you're generating viral traffic and engagement from your posts you have to understand the habits of the "typical" facebook user. They almost always see your posts in one of two ways.

> **Traffic Behavior Consistency #1 –** *"Sitting On FB And Just Saw This"*
>
> I think the title pretty much says it, but this is the 2nd most effective way to get viral traffic.
> Understand that many people will see a post "pop into their feed" while they are on facebook. So the

more times you post, the more often you get this type of traffic.

Traffic Behavior Consistency #2 – *"Just Logged In And Scrolling Through My Feed"*

This is where subtle photo tricks really come in to play. If you have a viral page, this will almost always be your most powerful form of traffic. When someone logs into their facebook for the first time for the day they usually start scrolling through their feed to catch up on what has happened since they logged in last. This makes things like stroking the photo in red, short punchy status updates, and LOUD photo's in general very important.

Now obviously this is going to vary a little bit. People are more willing to look at puppies all day than they will forex tips. But if you've chosen a social niche, or put some thought into making funny, and social photos, you'll get a lot further by posting a lot more.

Since the myth has been busted, you have another problem to deal with. You don't want to log in to facebook every hour to post something. Fortunately, facebook has a very simple automation feature built in to set this up for you.

Automation

It's really simple to schedule future posts, you can set them up as far as 6 months in advance. Simple choose the photo you want to upload, write your status update, then click the small clock icon you see in the bottom left of the above photo. In one day you could load up enough posts for a month and have all of your traffic completely automated.

Chapter 7) Tagenomics

Remember that yo-yo page I showed you an example of earlier?

It only had 2,015 fans on it, yet I still mentioned it to you. And that's because it just goes to show, with a little smart thinking, and a small fan base you can accomplish some great things within a community of people.

Here, check this out.

Now, I know you don't have a clue who these people are, but Gentry Stein is a national yo-yo champion and is famous all over this niche. He has people wearing T-shirts with his picture, thousands of yo-yo's sold every month with his name on it.

Imagine the exposure you can get for any brand like this?

Example: Snowboarding Niche

Status update: Who is your favorite snowboarding competitor?

(Vote, and tag them in the comments below)

Example: Local Restaurant

Status update: Who's your favorite person to drink with?

(Tag them in the comments below for a half price drink tonight!)

So you could probably start to see a few uses for this. Facebook is one powerful machine when used correctly, just because you don't have 100,000+ fans, doesn't mean you can't bring in a TON of business with a few proven strategies.

Chapter 8) Feeding The Viral Bait

When it comes to 'going viral" there isn't much luck to it. Sure you can have the fluke post here and there that seems to go viral for no apparent reason, but most every post that goes viral, is engineered to do so.

In 2011 Facebook changed from the "newsfeed" based fan pages and profiles to "timeline" based fan pages. This was huge change for niche-based pages. I know my passion niches like pit bulls, took a huge hit from this. People used to sit around on my page all day uploading their own photos to the newsfeed. Then, in April, Facebook said bye to the old pages, and hello to cover photos and timeline landers. Once this happened, you had to either get really good at making your posts go viral, or the interaction with your page would die.

For months I tested everything I could to send each and every post I did a little more viral. I added red to them, arrows, strokes, and effects, which all helped. I tried out different status update copy and found that short and punchy, with solid calls to action really crushed it. And when you put every little tweak together, you really start to manipulate the viral ranking factors for posts.

EDGErank Explained

EDGErank is the viral algorithm that facebook claims doesn't exist. Well, you can call it EDGErank, or you can call it whatever name you want, but the fact is that there is a ranking algorithm for who sees your posts. I can say this with 100% confidence because for every day of the last year and a half I have been manipulating the heck out of it.

How things go viral breaks down to three core viral ranking factors.

Viral Ranking Factor 1 – Affinity

Have you ever noticed that some of your friends always seem to show up on your newsfeed, while others barely ever seem to show? Well, the same thing happens with the fans of your fan page. Facebook has a ranking factor called "Affinity" that basically tells them how often someone engages with your post. So if you're constantly engaging with someone (usually your closest friends or favorite pages) facebook is going to take that as a sign to show your posts to that person more often.

Viral Ranking Factor 2 – Weight

Do you find it easier to hit "like" on something than to hit "share" and post it on your wall?

So does everybody else. Facebook assigns "weight" to the different actions someone takes on your post. So if a post is getting tons of comments, facebook is going to reward it more than likes. Shares will get rewarded even more due to the high visibility of it on people's timeline, and the weight it carries in the long-term virality algorithm.

Viral Ranking Factor 3 – Time Decay

Think of this as SPEED. The faster you can get people to interact with your post, the more viral it will go. Think about athletes when they post right after a game. People who just watched the game are going to reply with lightening speed. Facebook will reward you the faster you can get your fans to interact with your posts.

Once you start to truly understand the factors, you will start crafting status updates and posts that will play into that. And once you do, every single post on your page will reap the benefits. So to get you off on the right foot, here are a few tricks that you can use to leverage the algorithm.

Viral Ranking Manipulation Trick 1 – Time Decay Buster – "Help Us Reach "X,XXX" Likes"

---Example---

Help this photo get to 1,000 "likes" and we will have a cutest pit bull contest!

---End Example---

The way this works is by calling out a number of likes that you know for a fact you will hit quickly. If you set the number too high people are less likely to participate.

Viral Ranking Manipulation Trick 2 – Weight Pusher – "Photoshopped Or Not"

Photoshopped Or Not?

Once you post this, or a variance of this on your site, you'll instantly start getting comments from people who would normally not engage in your postings. I do this every so often on all of my pages, just to make sure I can get as much of my audience commenting and engaging as possible.

There are many tricks that you can use to leverage facebooks ranking factors, but at the end of the day, you need to post a lot and start thinking of how you can go "more viral" in every post you make. Winning on faecbook is about getting as many pieces of the "viral puzzle" right consistently post after post.

Chapter 9) Viral Visuals

Ok, so you just learned a ton of viral ranking tricks and pretty much how facebook ranks each post in terms of virality. Now, if you want to increase your virality and reach in everything you do on facebook you need to become a photo ninja. It's called facebook for a reason, it's about photos, so you better take time when you make your photos.

The Red Boat In A Blue Ocean Concept

Picture this.

Seriously picture this in your mind as you read this.

Imagine you are on vacation somewhere beautiful in the Carribean Sea at a nice hotel. You just checked in, it's the middle of the day, you walk into the room, put down your luggage, and slowly breathe in the air. Naturally, you walk out on to the balcony to look at the ocean. You look out and see a gorgeous ocean, beautiful, and vividly blue and glowing for as long as your eyes can see. There are huge white, black, and blue boats passing by, back and forth in the ocean, with people smiling and dancing on them. Then all the sudden, out of the corner of your eye, you see this tiny red sailing boat. With red sails, and only one person in it. Slowly sailing into your view. You immediately turn your head to see it.

Can you picture it?

Well that's how it is on facebook. Everything is in a blue border, and the last thing you want to do is post a blue photo because they blend in. Then, when people log in to facebook for the first time for the day and scroll up their feed to catch up on what they missed, they will completely miss yours. Overtime, that adds up to A LOT of traffic, so every photo you should do everything you can to make it stand out, even if it's small little tweaks.

Strokes

--- Great Photo For A Viral Post Example ---

--- Great Ad Photo Example ---

Pit Bulls

Click "like" if you LOVE
Pit Bulls!

You like Pit Bulls.

As you can see, that red border will catch your eye when everything else on facebook is blue. Ads are up in the top right corner of facebook, and everyone's main focus is on the newsfeed in the middle. So use red borders and experiment with slightly different photo sizes to try to further stand out.

Arrows

--- Viral Post With Arrow Example ---

This is an ugly photo, but it does work, because you can't help but see the word "LIKE?" and the arrow that would point directly at the like button. Since this photo has a very plain background without a lot of noise, this ugly box callout works really well, if it had skyscrapers in the background it wouldn't have quite the same effect.

--- Ad With Arrow Example ---

1 Ad

The picture quality probably isn't perfect on this one, but as you can see, that arrow points directly to where the like button would be on facebook. This always increases the CTR on ads and is worth testing out no matter what niche you're in, even local.

There are tons of things you can do to make your photo's stand out. You can add bubble callout's for caption contest photo's, add strokes, arrows, stretch effects, and tons more. Test things, and see what works for you, I am by no means a graphics expert, but no matter what you do, try and incorporate lots of red in it.

Chapter 10) Trend Trapping

Imagine for a moment you're a stock broker that has an inside tip and you know exactly when the stock is going to be at it's highest and you know exactly when it is going to tank. So, you know the perfect time to buy the stock at, sell the stock at, and then when to buy again at for maximum ROI. This is how trends are in facebook marketing.

If you can tap into a trending topic you can gain massive exposure on facebook almost overnight. I've done this with controversial political topics, predictable big events like the Olympics, and time and time again after big sporting events that are on PPV such as boxing and mixed martial arts.

Trends Example – Manny Pacquiao

Here is a perfect example of a predictable trend. Manny Pacquiao's fights are always on PPV and are seen by millions of people. I saw tons of successful pages sprout up in the boxing niche overnight. Just take a look at the rolling trends with predictable spikes every time he has a fight.

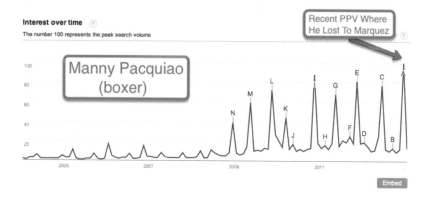

Every time he is going to have a fight, you see a spike. It's PREDICTABLE, just like the Olympics and any other event.

Google Trends

That graph above that I showed is from simply heading on over to http://trends.google.com and typing in whatever keyword I wanted to search for. It's a free service that is great to use for getting ideas of things and topics that go viral.

Here's an even more recent example involving Lance Armstrong.

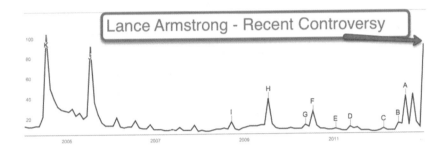

If you have followed Lance Armstrong at all, this trend graph would probably make a lot of sense to you. You have the spikes in the early years when he was winning all of those medals. Then the spikes when he had the steroid controversy, and then you have the final, huge spike, where he recently went on Oprah and told the world the truth about his steroid use.

I glance at trends at least a few times a week to see if anything sticks out to me that is super controversial that I could easily tap in to. I've actually got an entire course on this coming out in early February 2013.

Chapter 11) Successful Cloning Structures

Ok, for a moment I want you to imagine in your brain one word. Just imagine your favorite hobby. Whether it's playing football, gymnastics, juggling, exercising, etc. Just picture that word in your head. Now take that word on over to Google, and imagine the results that might pop-up. Now imagine that there was no Google ranking algorithm and you can put your website anywhere in the return search results you wanted.

Where would you put it?

OPTION 1 – Stick your website right at the top

Now this is the option that most people will instantly think of, and it's actually a good answer. I mean who doesn't want to be #1 on page one?

OPTION 2 – Be every listing on the page

Obvious right? Well very few people originally think of this, and that is because our brain as a marketer has been hard-wired to just think about being in one spot. Because SEO has takes so long, and it gets difficult to get all of your sites ranking on the same page. But this is still the better route to go with SEO.

There is no need to re-invent the wheel. Especially with facebook, there is no dinging you for duplicate content, that's just not how facebook works. Once you've found ads that work, run them again to a similar page. You've already done all the hard work finding a winning niche, don't go searching for a new one, just expand your reach with multiple pages. I've got like 4 pit bulls pages, and that's just one niche.

Also, you may want to go a step further when you are spreading out your net and build more of a community by starting a group. There are tons of these sprouting up in the marketing community already and I have a feeling that they are only going to get more popular every day.

Group Example – Pit Bulls

(Note: To create a group: https://www.facebook.com/about/groups/)

As you can see, that group grows all by itself and is extremely active. Someone posts in it every day, and every post gets tons of engagement. I can change it at any time to where only the admins post, and everyone in there still gets the alert, and goes to check what I just posted. This is very powerful for local when used in conjunction with a contest. If you're not using groups, you're missing out on generating a real bond with your following.

Chapter 12) Putting It All Together

Even though this book wasn't that long, I know I threw a lot at you at once. You learned a little bit about demographic research, proper PPC campaigns, and how to go viral. So it's time we did a recap on exactly what is going on here so that you know what to do.

The "Big Picture" Sequence

Step 1) Write Down Your Niche Ideas

Step 2) Run Them Through A Viral Checklist

> Is It Big Enough?
> Is It Evergreen?
> Is There Passion?
> Is There A Sense Of Community?
> Is There Controversy?

(Note: you don't need every one of these, but each helps)

Step 3) Run A Quick "Like" Campaign For Initial Traffic

Step 4) Watch Your Ads

Step 5) Dial In Your Ad Campaigns

Step 6) Start Going Viral With Well Crafted Photos And Posts

Step 7) Start Sending Out Affiliate Links, Links To Opt-in To Your Promotion List, Or However You Profit

Step 8) Automate 1 Week Of Posts

Step 9) Clone Yourself In A Successful Niche

Step 10) Repeat

That's it!

You're now armed with more information on facebook marketing than 99% of marketers out there. I hope you really enjoyed all the information in this book. If you'd like to get more information on facebook marketing head to http://marketingwithdon.com/bookgift/ and download the free gift as my way of saying thanks for reading this awesome book. (You're going to love the gift)

Now get out there, go download that gift, and then get started on building a viral fan page. You have all the information, now go take action.

See you at the top,

-don

Printed in Great Britain
by Amazon.co.uk, Ltd.,
Marston Gate.